Developmental psychology for beginners

How to easily understand the stages of development from infant to adult and apply the insights specifically to your life or child rearing

Maria Kiemer

CONTENT

What you can expect in this guide

Who are we? Or perhaps more accurately, why are we who we are? That depends on whom you ask, but most people will agree that our identity is largely determined by our experiences. This includes personal highlights, such as first love, but also personal crises and dealing with our deepest fears. Basically, what matters most to our personal journey through life is the strategies we use to master such very special challenges in the first place. When we are successful, to what factors do we attribute this success - our own ability or mere luck? When we are stuck in a crisis, do we prefer to sit on our helplessness or do we ask someone for help?

You may now be surprised to learn that such questions revolve less around the individual than they might seem. How we deal with conflict has to do, above all, with who we learn from and who we can rely on completely. Developmental psychology is concerned with precisely such questions and with what we can best do from a scientific perspective both to accompany children on their journey through life and to understand and ultimately master our own life crises.

In this guidebook, you will gain an easy-to-understand overview of modern developments in developmental psychology and the extent to which they can be applied to your personal everyday life. You will then receive a guide that will help you understand what particularly concerns a person at what point in their life from a psychological point of view, and actionable tips on how to offer a helping hand. Whether you want to understand why your daughter seems so upset lately, or you're feeling a bit at a loss at the moment and would like a fresh perspective on your life from the outside - with this guide, the human psyche will seem more crystal clear than ever before.

What is meant by "development"?

EARLIER RESEARCH VS. CURRENT STATUS

Developmental psychology is a scientific discipline that describes and attempts to explain different aspects of human behavior and experience. The central question is why people develop differently and how these developmental processes can be systematized. Developmental psychology is primarily concerned with child development and works closely with other disciplines that offer overlaps in this aspect, for example with educational science and neuroscience. For this reason, there are several explanatory approaches that combine sociological and biological assumptions.

Classic disputes in developmental psychology deal, for example, with the question of whether our development is influenced more by our genetic endowments or by our environment *(nature vs. nurture)*. Most modern developmental psychologists agree that both factors play important roles. Various studies of twins support the assumption that genetics already determines many things from the beginning. Identical twins given up for adoption at birth and adopted by different households have been the subject of many years of research, which observed the children as they developed and compared the results once the twins, now adults, contacted each other. Shocking parallels emerged in their biographies, such as similar fashion preferences, similar friendship constellations, or similar career choices that could not be explained by mere coincidences. On the other hand, children are significantly influenced by the parental home and their wider social environment in which they grow up. How children deal with conflicts and to what extent they are able to maintain relationships is something they learn in their interactions with their parents and early childhood friends. Famous experiments in developmental psychology, for example, involved observing two-year-olds in stressful situations to see whether they immediately sought reassurance from an adult or faced a new situation with confidence and curiosity.

Over time, moreover, an adolescent's priorities[1] are oriented toward the priorities that are modeled for them. A particularly striking experiment in developmental psychology could be observed in the case of the Hungarian sisters Judit, Zsófia and Zsuzsa Polgár, who received chess lessons from their parents Klara and László Polgár as children in the mid-1970s. The Polgár couple assumed that geniuses were not born, but educated.

They chose chess as a subject because, unlike in art or music, progress and strategies made in this field could be calculated mathematically. None of them possessed a pronounced talent for chess, but they did have a deep enthusiasm for the game. All three sisters grew up to be top chess players, reaching the profoundly male ranks of the chess elite. Each of the sisters later emphasized that their upbringing had focused on the fun of the game, which ultimately motivated them to devote extra time to their hobby.

---

[1] In this guide, the masculine form is mostly used as a general designation for better comprehensibility. Of course, all designations apply to all people, unless otherwise stated.

These early practice sessions on a voluntary basis enabled a high level of experience to be gained at an early age and paved the way to the top of the world. The Polgárs had thus succeeded in making a decisive argument that "child prodigies" ostensibly become experts in their field through their upbringing, and that children merely need to be given good stimuli in order to develop their full abilities. Both factors, genetics and actual education, thus complement each other and must be taken into account in child rearing from both a developmental psychology and a pedagogical point of view.

A second popular controversy in developmental psychology is whether we should rather speak of a phased or a stepwise development in terms of human development. Let us explain this a little more clearly by means of an example: Imagine that you go for a walk in the forest every Sunday, always choosing the same path. One day you notice a small spruce.

In the following years, you follow the growth of this spruce. Of course, it gains in girth and size, it may develop a fuller needle splendor, but nevertheless it remains at its core the same spruce that you originally discovered. Developmental psychologists understand this to mean *continuous development* - no dramatic upheavals take place, the tree merely gains strength. It's different, for example, with butterflies that hatch as caterpillars, go through a pupal stage, and leave their cocoon as adult butterflies. In this case, developmental psychologists speak of *discontinuous development* because two clearly identifiable upheavals have occurred in the butterfly's appearance and behavior. What do you think is the developmental process that humans go through? And before you spontaneously decide on one possibility, pause for a moment. Is sexual maturity now mere growth or a dramatic upheaval? What about mental development, which was not addressed at all in either example? When we speak of dramatic upheavals, at what point in our development do we best locate them? Are you still the same person at the core that you were 20 years ago?

Most notable developmental psychologists established models based on phased and sequential development. Before the 20th century, renowned thinkers such as Jean-Jacques Rousseau addressed the tension between independence and well-meaning guidance, from which a growing child should benefit equally. The idea of the kindergarten, in which children literally learn how to grow and develop intellectually, also emerged from this era. However, it was not until along with the rising influence of psychology on the humanities and natural sciences in the early 20th century that a real foothold for developmental psychology could be established.

Now it was possible to formulate concrete hypotheses that could be tested by psychological experiments.

Karl Bühler, who taught at the Technical University of Dresden during this period, developed one of the first modern age typologies for children. Like later developmental psychologists, he based his phase delineation on observable activities that children mainly pursue at different ages - newborn *infants* are fixated on feeding, toddler *runners* enthusiastically pursue their growing mobility, and preschoolers live out their fantasies and curiosities in social interactions with each other at *story age*. In Jean Piaget's four-part theory of cognitive development, which was influenced by epistemological-philosophical approaches, children acquire initial motor coordination and develop conceptions of objects as well as gradually the ability to think logically, which they demonstrate to varying degrees depending on their stage of development. Children must first be able to distinguish between animate and inanimate objects as well as understand the concept of the abstract, for example addition tasks, before they can logically solve more complex problems. Piaget verified his theses by means of practical experiments involving children, and for this reason he continues to enjoy a certain esteem in psychological and educational circles. Both models have already been criticized for speaking of clearly delineated phases, when in fact they should speak of smooth transitions.

Looking at the human brain, it should be clear why our development should be viewed more like an elevator than a staircase. Neural networks are characterized by constant re-linking, which degrades when neglected. The earlier you start practicing a particular skill, the larger - read: better connected - the brain areas in question become. This is mainly because young brains are more malleable and absorb new information two to three times better on average than older brains (see Baltes & Kliegl, 1992). Because any learning process is based on existing knowledge, expanded knowledge structures facilitate the learning of related but new information and skills. However, when these knowledge structures fall victim to, for example, disease or accidents, it is not necessarily the case that the individual automatically regresses to a previous stage of development. In 2011, the U.S. politician Gabby Giffords was the victim of a terrorist attack in which a pistol bullet penetrated one of her cerebral hemispheres. Her salvation was that the bullet missed the other hemisphere of her brain. As a result, she lost her ability to speak, but not her ability to reason or her past memories. Her musical abilities had also remained intact. She retrained her speech ability through long, hard work. In 2020, she gave a live speech that proved what a long way she had come since the attempt on her life.

If you follow Buehler's or Piaget's model, it should be clear that Giffords was never really at the level of a toddler - she had merely lost the neural networks necessary to do so and then rebuilt them one-on-one. Challenges we had at an earlier point in our development can arise again at any time. Humans are amazing products of nature and can overcome some of these challenges without losing their maturity as adults.

Developmental psychology is an exceedingly broad field and cannot be presented in its full scope in this guidebook. Most experiments deal with early childhood education and, in its context, with the development of motivation, expectancies, and learning strategies. Research in the 21st century focuses instead on lifelong development and learning processes and now includes the role of multimedia influences, i.e., television and the Internet, in its hypotheses around human development. Various models have been expanded and redeveloped to make room for the role of moral education and individual character traits.

Furthermore, it is now questioned whether we can apply uniform models to all people regardless of their generation and cultural background - recent findings indicate that this may lead to some misconceptions. Comparisons between European and Asian parenting styles, for example, have shown that the role of individuality plays a much less important role in Asian households than in the West. This is not to say that in these cultures the individual as such is despised; rather, a stronger interpersonal relationship is felt between oneself and the family to which one belongs.

The needs of the family have a special role and it tends not to be seen as a great personal sacrifice to compromise in order to fulfill these family needs. In contrast, European and other Westernized cultures tend to be much more focused on the differences between oneself and the environment. Individuals define themselves by what sets them apart from others and celebrate this difference as something special. Such influences need to be taken into account in developmental psychology so that appropriate new approaches can accommodate the diverse approaches to education around the world.

Each generation is also shaped by a drastic event or a new technology, whether it is living through a pandemic or the development of the smartphone. Linguists point out that our individual native language has a lasting impact on our general understanding of language and our emotionality. Ideographic research is primarily interested in differences in child development and is finding increasingly better application on newer foundations. It is likely that many more discoveries await us in deciphering human development.

WHY THE ERIKSON MODEL CONTINUES TO BE A GOOD GUIDE

If postmodern developmental psychology challenges most previous models, why am I introducing you below to a model first published in 1950? Aren't there now more modern models that address, for example, the lasting impact of the Internet on our development? Of course there are. The problem is that the models in question usually focus on one main influence on development, but neglect other aspects. Some models are dominated by the socio-political context in which a person matures, while others take as their starting point the inner virtues that people possess.

Although developmental psychology benefits from its many intersections with education and various humanities, such models serve more as a support to show us that human development is an extremely complex, lifelong process. It is more useful to use a model that allows for both psychological and sociological approaches. Erik Erikson's stage model of psychosocial development is one such model and a popular starting point for more modern theories for this very reason. Although it is one of the more aged explanatory approaches, it has received its well-deserved attention only in recent decades and, just like modern ideas, it covers the entire spectrum of life.

Erik Erikson was a German-American psychoanalyst who had contact with theories of psychology during his studies. Together with his wife Joan Serson, he developed the common stage model, which differs drastically from his original influences, namely Sigmund Freud. Freud's research focused primarily on a popularized notion of early childhood sexual tendencies, fixations, and neuroses. While today it is conceded that Freud did a good job of elaborating the role of the unconscious, there is criticism particularly of sexual neuroses, which he believed to be instrumental in all early childhood development. Erikson also took exception to Freud's assumption that personality development should end by the age of five - he saw clearer arguments that childhood lasts much longer and that even adults go through various stages of personal development in future situations.

While Freud viewed human development rather from a clinical and pessimistic point of view because he considered personalities unchangeable, Erikson opened the field for optimism through his idea of lifelong development; mistakes made earlier can later be logically analyzed and avoided, even become the trigger for a sense of achievement. The later extension of Freudian psychology placed special emphasis on the so-called ego psychology, in which the ego and its relationship to its environment come to the fore. Erikson's theory is closely related to the latter field. His theses continue to be readily taken up and further developed today:

• In their development, human beings go through mainly psychosocial phases, i.e. their mental and cognitive abilities are learned and practiced in interaction with others.

• Everyone deals with eight core conflicts throughout their lives, which help them gain new insights about themselves and others and give them the skills they need to deal with future conflicts.

• In early childhood, unlike adults, humans are not at all able to perceive and evaluate objects correctly. Childhood is thus defined as the absence of abilities, which are gradually acquired and mastered through increasingly complex and differentiated processes.

• The most important phase of development is puberty, during which a particularly large number of internal and external conflicts are played out.

• Childhood is characterized by the gradual acquisition of skills.

• The developmental process is predominantly shaped by the genes present, but environmental factors such as the immediate family just as cultures and technologies influence the nature as well as the management of various conflicts. Erikson acknowledges that different cultures also affect the developmental process differently. Nevertheless, he says that each of us follows "inner laws" that help determine our approach to social interactions and, accordingly, allow for cross-cultural parallels between different parenting styles.

• A healthy personality of a person consists of an active influence on his environment, the acceptance of all his own character traits, and a realistic view of himself and his environment. Each of these three traits is linked to another - for example, in order to actively influence my environment, I need to have a realistic view of myself in the first place, that is, to have confidence in my own abilities and an understanding of the circumscribed role I play in my environment. For example, it is unhealthy for me to proudly stand up and chop down the entire supply of wood for the winter when I have no strength in my arms at all. In turn, a realistic assessment of my own abilities leads more easily to acceptance of my own faults and shortcomings

- I may not be the best woodchopper in the house, but I am a pretty good cook. Not only does it make much more sense from a practical point of view to distance yourself from challenges that are too great, but it's also better for your own psyche in the long run.

• Personality development is a lifelong process. At every stage, a person can learn something new, no matter how old and experienced they are.

For this guidebook, Erikson's model was chosen as a guideline, which overlaps with other findings in psychology. The individual phases cannot be clearly distinguished from one another, because Erikson assumes a development that merges into one another. In the following chapter, you will gain insight into a person's psyche, from birth to old age, in short, understandable sketches. I recommend that you read each section, as some conflicts may recur throughout life. Each section contains two to three tips that will help you find coping strategies for any age-whether you want to develop a better understanding of your child's development or wonder what developmental psychological insights might be useful to yourself at the current point in your life.

From toddler to adult - what moves us internally

INFANCY: PRIMORDIAL TRUST VS. PRIMORDIAL MISTRUST

We begin, how could it be otherwise, at the very beginning - or at least directly after the birth of a child. What drastic experiences a child has in *the* womb still remains a well-kept secret. The fact is: no human life begins in total loneliness. The act of giving birth is a drastic experience for both the mother and the child she gives birth to. Have you ever wondered why it is recommended that the newborn get direct skin-to-skin contact with its parents as soon as possible?

In addition to the extremely beneficial release of parental hormones, the child's psyche in particular is supported. Newborns can neither see nor hear particularly well, but they respond all the better to human warmth and especially to the pulse, the muffled sound of which they still know from their time in utero. The most important thing for a brand-new and completely disoriented human being is to be able to hold on to something that is as familiar as possible. This is the first major crisis a person must face in his life: He must develop the ability to trust, so that his encounter with new experiences is not accompanied in the long run by fundamental distrust. More difficult said than done! What possibilities do you yourself have as an adult to place your trust in strange people or situations? Perhaps you believe in the Golden Rule and deepen your relationship through direct contact with each other. Or maybe you are more skeptical and first gather information about this unfamiliar situation, for example, by talking to your friends or researching online for several hours. Maybe you keep your options as open as possible and always have a plan B ready in case someone actually betrays your trust. Now try to put yourself in the position of an infant. This one has no idea whatsoever about morals or good etiquette. He is equally unable to offer anything in return for a good turn or to escape a frightening situation on his own. In the first year of life, his ability to communicate is limited to crying, with which he simultaneously communicates his needs and asks for help.

In this phase, every call of the infant is to be understood as an *all in* - he relies completely on the hope that his caregivers will show attention and take care of his worries. At the same time, he thus learns that his voice is literally heard and that he has a direct influence on his environment. Thus, his worries are alleviated and he can learn to accept his temporary dependence as such. "Hope" is the main ingredient in teaching a child to trust, so that the child can show that trust to someone in the future. This trust, in turn, is the mental foundation for every learning process and emotional relationship the child will later enter into. If a child cannot develop trust, he or she will feel completely helpless in crisis situations and will never be able to see the good in others; most importantly, he or she will not be able to see the good in himself or herself.

<u>What is particularly helpful at this stage:</u>

✓ **Give your child as stable a sense of security as possible.** If your child seeks contact with you, you should be receptive and reliable to that contact. This means not letting your child "cry it out." Contrary to popular advice for young parents, this does not teach an infant to self-soothe. Much more likely, the lesson learned is for the infant to be left alone with his or her problems. So at this particularly sensitive stage of life, show that you can and always will respond when your child expresses such a need.

✓ **Take your child's fears seriously.** Infants cannot express in a differentiated way which worries are really urgent (full diapers) and which worries are not (a big shadow on the wall). Anyway, it would be advisable for you to try to see every fear from your child's perspective. Almost every experience is new and alienating, and it is a matter of learning to deal with it. Most problems do not call for an overly complicated solution, but every problem does call for dealing with it. Show your child that none of his worries are beneath you as a caregiver.

EARLY CHILDHOOD: AUTONOMY VS. SELF-DOUBT

Between a toddler's first and third birthday, another question dominates his inner life, namely the question of his own autonomy or independence. The toddler has learned how the environment reacts to his helplessness. In the meantime, it has developed its own abilities - and among the most important of these new abilities is undoubtedly the ability to regulate its own outbursts. Whoever is rudimentarily familiar with Sigmund Freud's theories will be able to discover a parallel to the anal phase at this point. In this respect, this parallel is justified, since a more mature musculature is accompanied by a better understanding of (self-)control. However, exercising control also means being able to feel shame.

"Shame" always has something to do with the process of letting go, whether it literally involves physical excretions or else verbal expressions. After all, something embarrassing can literally "slip out" at any age. In this respect, therefore, the young child develops a particularly deep relationship with his own body, since a lack of control over his bodily functions immediately leads to feelings of shame. This shame does not set in only after the actual mishap, but also dominates in advance: what might happen if I lose my self-control later? What might I have to fear? Even long after independent toileting has been learned, such thought patterns may surface in adults. Some of us are consumed by fears that make us shrink inside, give us stomach cramps, and cause us to doubt ourselves.

Those who learn to deal with such impulses as early as possible will have a much better chance of dealing with feelings of insecurity later on.

What is trained here is the ability of willpower. Toddlers need a clear balance between authority and flexibility from their parents at this stage in order to develop confidence and trust in their own abilities.

What is particularly helpful at this stage:

✓ **Tread with firmness.** While a child is developing its first autonomy, it must at the same time have an authority to which it can turn when necessary. This is where you lay the foundation for your child to recognize and respect authority as such. You want to be an authority your child trusts and can turn to when he or she is in danger of overstepping boundaries. In this way, it learns to take responsibility for its actions and to deal with mishaps.

✓ **Show your flexible and patient side.** The muscles of the body are as complicated an instrument as the interplay of pride and shame. Develop an understanding that learning autonomy takes time and room for failure, and take a step-by-step approach with your child rather than leaps and bounds.

PRESCHOOL AGE: INITIATIVE VS. GUILT

Around the age of three, a child usually develops the need for a goal that he or she can reach through his or her own efforts. If you take a look at the two previous phases, this makes perfect sense: help from others as well as self-help have ideally been learned by now, the child knows how to express himself and move independently - now it's time to put these skills to the test.

Especially in exchanges with peers, what happens with siblings or in kindergarten, for example, wishes and hopes are now discussed animatedly and measured against each other. The child's imagination really blossoms in this environment, but can get out of hand under certain circumstances. Ideas may emerge that frighten the child himself because he has already thought or dreamed of them. It is the heyday of nocturnal monsters and the horror of one's own possibilities of action. Suddenly there are anxious questions about what is good and what is evil; whether I am a bad person if I do evil; whether my friends will continue to love me if I have already *thought* of something evil ...

So at this age, children develop a deeper understanding of "right" and "wrong" and become aware that they may well do things that are later understood to be wrong. This idea makes them feel guilty. In order to set a goal, the child must be able to overcome these feelings of guilt in order to tackle more difficult situations with clear self-confidence.

<u>What is particularly helpful at this stage:</u>
✓ **Instill confidence and calm in your child.** You have a far better perspective on the interplay between right and wrong than your five-year-old can have at this point. You provide the emotional counterbalance, thereby enabling your child to better process stressful situations.

✓ **Make consequences understandable and avoidable.** It is important that your child understands: boundaries exist in order to develop a moral compass in the first place. If he does something wrong, for example, taking away his best friend's dessert, consequences for this wrong behavior must be expected. Of course, your child wants to avoid unpleasant consequences and will act accordingly. However, by remaining objective and disclosing the connection between changeable behavior and consequences, your child will be able to distance himself from his actions. He will understand that his self-esteem remains unchanged and that he has complete control over his actions. Thus, it develops a growing self-confidence and builds the ability to take responsibility for itself.

ELEMENTARY SCHOOL AGE: COMPETENCE VS. INFERIORITY

From the point of view of developmental psychology, this stage of life is viewed with varying degrees of importance - according to Erikson, it is only now that a truly fundamental development of a person's personality takes place. Skills and competencies that are developed and practiced now can best develop later. From about the age of six, i.e. often together with entry into elementary school, children begin to emerge from their fantasy world. They now place greater emphasis on creating something "real," i.e., completing certain things and thereby gaining satisfaction and recognition. This recognition should come not only from parents, teachers and friends, but is also an internal process in which the child learns to appreciate his or her own abilities.

Of course, recognition is easier to recognize from the outside, especially due to the fact that children at this age are familiarized with success evaluations for the first time. They now receive school grades, so their successes and failures are assessed for all to see. This leads to a better understanding of what makes a project successful or unsuccessful, but at the same time also to a certain internal pressure. A C is understood by the child not only as a "mediocre" performance in itself, but also as a mediocre performance within the class structure itself. Educators also understand this development under the concept of the *social reference norm*, in which the child is measured not ostensibly by his individual development, but by his classmates. Some children like such competitive situations and show particular ambition when they have the opportunity to shine in a comparison against their friends. However, it is important that they always appreciate their own development and be patient with themselves when they need more time to find solutions to problems.

This sounds like a stressful situation - but if the child has learned trust, autonomy and self-confidence in the preceding developmental phases, he or she will be able to deal with this stress appropriately and will not want to hang his or her self-esteem on mere school grades. Even in adulthood, at all, the way we seek solutions to a problem is an auto-matic statement of confidence in ourselves. You know that feeling where you think something has no point at all anyway? Why tackle something when it probably won't turn out well enough anyway? Such an attitude then makes us procrastinate, which only makes the problem in question seem bigger and more difficult.

A child, on the other hand, who invests time and effort in his projects is a child who believes in his own abilities. The focus is not on the thought of possible failure, but on an orientation in the direction of what is feasible and what can be achieved in what time, realistically speaking. At this age, you will be able to see up close whether your child is developing into an optimist or more of a pessimist. This attitude is strongly related to the extent to which your child believes that he or she can bring about and change something through his or her own efforts.

What is particularly helpful at this stage:

✓ **Place special emphasis on your child's individual development. Children** already feel the external pressure to fit into their class community and perform well. Ask about what your child has learned for himself and how he wants to deal with (previous) failures. If you notice that your child is struggling in class, this is not automatically a reason to panic. Your child may be developing a different skill or may need to see the problem from several angles first to be able to solve it. What is crucial is that your child learns to be patient with himself and sees his learning process as something that is enjoyable and rewards you for your effort.

✓ **Have realistic expectations.** Children benefit most when they sense that you are attentive to their learning process. Underestimating your child's abilities ("This is way too difficult for you!") may lead to feelings of inferiority, while overestimating ("You'll be able to do it in no time!") may in turn make the child feel intimidated and overwhelmed. Therefore, don't expect your child to be equally successful in every school subject and at every stage of life. If your child shows confidence and ambition in one school subject, demonstrate your confidence and trust - if he or she feels insecure in another subject and has a history of failure, show empathy and support. This way, your child knows that you are actively following his or her learning process, but that at the same time, he or she does not have to fear disappointment on your part.

PUBERTY: IDENTITY VS. ROLE DIFFUSION

Around the end of elementary school, a child has initially learned how to deal with evaluative situations and how to react to stress. With the onset of puberty, it now becomes clearly more important again what place it takes in a group and how strong its relationships are with friends and perhaps even enemies. It is not without reason that the pubertal brain is called a real construction site!

At this age, the human brain develops myriads of new brain connections and then cuts a good portion again; some brain areas develop earlier and faster, while others might as well be in a little ice age. Fewer connections remain than at the beginning, but these transport information at a higher speed. This process is also called neuronal Darwinism, because the brain establishes with it which brain connections will play a more or important role in the future.

The prefrontal brain, for example, is particularly affected, which is why adolescents usually have a very hard time organizing their work schedules and completing tasks on time. His sense of time undergoes an immediate renovation during this phase. An adolescent may be less lazy for this reason, he just doesn't know how to mentally assess urgent and necessary tasks the way you might. He makes important decisions differently than you do: not with the help of his prefrontal brain, but still especially with the help of his amygdala, which is much more responsible for instinctive decisions. While these don't necessarily lead to bad outcomes, adolescents don't factor the possibility of negative consequences into their decision-making process. For this reason, saying "I didn't think about that!" is much closer to the truth than you might want to take from a teen in this situation. It makes more sense to show youth immediate bonuses for actions taken rather than placing a possible threat in the distant future. Rewards must also be higher because adolescents are neurologically less responsive to rewards than adults. This explains why adolescents sometimes take higher risks in order to be rewarded by their own brains with feelings of happiness in the first place.

Speech and spatial orientation are similarly brutally affected. Between the ages of twelve and eighteen, adolescents are only able to recognize the feelings of their fellow human beings to a limited extent, which explains why some seem so completely absorbed in their own emotional world. Discovering one's own sexuality may lead to great confusion and uncertainty. Do I even want to be found attractive, and if so, by whom? Do I find this person attractive at all? Do I want to be an adult already, with all the disadvantages that adulthood brings? In other words, the adolescent brain is in chaos, and yet it has to do cognitive as well as emotional heavy lifting. At this point, earlier conflicts are revisited and reevaluated: can I really trust my family and friends? Is there perhaps something about me that I should be ashamed of? Am I capable enough to achieve certain things, or am I perhaps not meeting school and social requirements? This is by no means a step back into childhood, but a necessary step so that the leap into adulthood can succeed. An adolescent is no longer a child who depends on blind faith for survival. He now has a greater wealth of experience, has a more complex view of the world, and knows that he must renegotiate his relationships. At this point, he must take up all his inner conflicts and reconcile them so that tangible expectations, fears, hopes, in other words, an identity, can develop from them. Young people now understand that the way they deal with problems and crises is comparable to the way adults deal with their own problems and crises.

The great inner challenge in this phase is that the understanding of social roles is not stable enough. Young people doubt who they are and what they mean to others. For this reason, they orient themselves to certain roles, which are prescribed and modeled for them, and define themselves through various groups to which they (want to) belong. Such social groups demonstrate their cohesion to the outside world by pursuing very specific external commonalities, e.g., through fashion trends, linguistic patterns or hairstyles, and by confirming their internal cohesion, for example, through shared enemy images and intolerance of outsiders.

For this reason, young people also seek conflict with those who are actually close to them, such as family members and childhood friends, because they may not belong to the youth subculture about which they identify so strongly. If confidants are suddenly chosen as opponents, this is mainly because an adolescent needs this conflict to see himself in the mirror and develop a sense of his own identity. At this age, adolescents want to know above all to whom and for what reason they want to be loyal. To do this, they first need to develop an understanding of what constitutes their personality and what personal boundaries must not be crossed in order to maintain a mutual relationship of trust.

<u>What is particularly helpful at this stage:</u>

✓ **Maintain the stability that is already familiar to your adolescent.** In crisis situations, we need an anchor that we can hold on to and that gives us orientation. In this case, that means sticking to regular and familiar routines. Such routines include, for example, fixed rituals such as shared dinners or times when your child should be asleep. Of course, you have to take into account that sixteen-year-olds like to spend time with their friends or, biologically speaking, get tired much later than their ten-year-old sister. So choose which existing rituals and rules you want to emphasize according to your family situation. It is important that your child perceives his or her home as a place of stability where certain consequences and contact persons are expected.

✓ **Allow your adolescent enough space to deal with inner conflicts.** Accept that at this point in developmental psychology, you must allow your particular position as an authority figure to be questioned. Adolescents place special importance on what opinions their friends and peers hold, and these will undoubtedly conflict with your own opinions. Adolescents must have physical and emotional places of retreat where they can think through and process their inner conflicts. So there must also be certain things that are beyond your immediate control. Respond with dignity and patience and show your child that you trust him. That way, he knows you take his more mature needs seriously and will be more likely to turn to you when he feels doubt or uncertainty.

✓ **Teach your adolescent that he or she can differ from group opinions.** Group affiliations are likely to change several times during human life, and cliques thrive on both external and internal conflict. Adolescents must learn that they can remain friends even if they see things as having different importance and their opinions do not coincide one hundred percent. This is an important prerequisite for developing tolerance for people outside one's own group and being able to live with differences. However, as a parent, you are not exempt from this! Tolerate your child's appropriate criticism of you. In this way, it learns that all authority must make transparent decisions in order to demand respect. Your relationship will be strengthened by how you handle differences of opinion that arise.

Mirror back to your child that this is how he or she can hold his or her own opinions and identity while receiving support and appreciation.

YOUNG ADULTHOOD: IDENTITY VS. ISOLATION

Once puberty is complete (which, by the way, can last into our early twenties), we talk about adulthood. At eighteen, we are legally completely responsible for ourselves and enjoy the freedom, but also the burden, of our choices. Be it first job experiences, deeper romantic relationships, or the actual life path we now want to take ... with this phase of life come concrete challenges that show we also have to grow into our adult lives. This new self-discovery phase lasts well into our 40s. From a technical point of view, the following three life phases leave the traditional ground of developmental psychology, because this rather refers to child and adolescent development. However, it would be a big mistake to consider the human relationship as finished with puberty. Even with a strong sense of one's own identity, human beings repeatedly go through inner crises that put their decisions and personal relationships to the test.

This phase of life reveals whether the previous conflicts have been overcome - because it is only through trust, autonomy, confidence and loyalty that an adult can feel and build intimacy. Healthy, intimate relationships consist of adults sharing their lives with each other without feeling that their identities are at risk. Those who have a strong identity of their own, according to Erikson's research, are more able to establish healthy sexual and/or intellectual intimacy and defend it against external threats. Friendships that do not have any romantic component should also feel addressed by this description. The keywords "intimacy" and "love" are quite crucial ingredients for building enduring and forgiving friendships in adulthood.

In psychology, there are divergent positions as to what is formed first, one's own identity or the capacity for intimacy. The U.S. psychologist Harry Stack Sullivan, for example, assumed that we first develop our identity on the basis of our relationships with other people, which Erikson places more clearly in the preceding developmental phase of adolescence. What both agree on is the fact that personal development cannot be accomplished alone. We are dependent on other people for this.

The capacity for intimacy is the direct prerequisite for being able to feel and show a sense of love. According to Erikson, love is our ability to accept another person in his or her difference. Unlike mere affection, which always seeks commonality, love can only arise from insight into and appreciation for the differences between oneself and the other. Love also consists in the ability to put our own needs in the background in order to meet the needs of the other, while at the same time understanding and respecting individual limits. Those who do not learn this skill will always perceive others as a threat, even when they should be among our intimates. In response to this threat, the individual withdraws into his or her own identity and shies away from leaving familiar territory - even when this withdrawal may keep one from genuine intimacy and love.

<u>What is particularly helpful at this stage:</u>

✓ **Take risks.** Getting involved with another person takes some courage and a willingness to make mistakes. At this point, you should have a sense of your own needs and know that failed relationships say nothing about your overall quality as a person. However, you can't gain anything without taking a chance. Be ready to discover the attraction of the other in your partner and understand possible conflicts as a chance to mature with each other.

✓ **Distinguish between surmountable and in-surmountable differences.** If you want to build true intimacy, it must not mean completely neglecting your own desires for the sake of the other person. A mature relationship means making compromises, and compromises must not be made permanently at the expense of one person. If you feel the need to talk about your concerns, but your partner shuts himself off from them and silently denies his problems, your joint communication will be affected. Determine which differences between you and your partner are wanted and accepted, and which differences threaten to undermine your relationship. Discuss these in mutual trust with your partner to see if these differences are really in-surmountable.

MATURE ADULTHOOD: GENERA-TIVITY VS. STAGNATION

With middle age, i.e. from about the age of 40 until retirement, one can speak of mature adulthood. The term "generativity" means the ability to help others in their own crises and to support them with wise advice. This requires a solidified sense of self and a wealth of life experiences gained in the process of successes and failures. This also includes mature sexual experiences and the ability to fully satisfy the sexual as well as romantic needs of one's partner.

Regardless of his or her own profession, the adult thus becomes a teacher and contact person for younger generations and inspires them to new insights. It is precisely at this point that it becomes apparent whether the ability for intimacy has been mastered beforehand, because the combination of different personalities results in the best possible stability and the largest pool of problem solutions that can be offered. This is particularly evident after starting a family, when the needs of young children put the couple in question to the test in a special way. A foundation for self-image is then laid, which is only called into question again when the children leave home for good and one has to reinvent oneself outside of one's role as a parent. However, this also applies to people who do not have children or partners and come into contact with younger generations in everyday life. In principle, it is possible for everyone and even beneficial for their psyche if they have the opportunity to inspire younger people and pick up new impulses through younger people. Those who cannot find this stimulation on an everyday basis have the option, for example, of taking an evening course or doing voluntary work - the main thing is to leave your usual routine from time to time and be prepared to learn something new.

By the term stagnation we mean a standing still and dwelling on our own problems. Those who show no readiness for intimacy cannot be in regular exchange with other points of view and therefore insist on their own convictions as the only acceptable solutions. Those who stagnate in their development can accordingly pass on less of their wealth of experience and enrich it just as little with new thought-provoking impulses. Stagnant adults often perceive themselves as deconstructive, because they also receive significantly less positive feedback due to their lack of willingness to share. Without looking ahead, they lack a certain future orientation that could give them enough self-confidence to age gracefully. One might also see this phase in connection with a reemerging debilitation:

Although you have gained a lot of experience and learned your lessons from it, you are increasingly losing influence on the lives of your children or on colleagues who are now maturing into stable adults themselves. Perhaps one's body is now giving one a hard time due to age and one is aware that one will be dependent on the help of others in the foreseeable future. For this reason, it is all the more important to look to the future with confidence and to know which relationships you can rely on in your own crisis situation.

<u>What is particularly helpful at this stage:</u>

✓ **Think of your role as a counselor only as a part-time job.** You are now taking on an important role in your social fabric as a (grand)parent who likes to be asked for help. Be aware, however, that advice is all the more likely to be valued if it is given only when asked. You should act as an authority whose judgment is not feared but respected. Also, be open to new suggestions, even if they come from people whose life experience may be less than yours. You are the unique result of your complex relationships, crises, and personal beliefs, so other perspectives are equally unique and may thus provide you with insights that would otherwise have been closed to you. Remember to insist on your own needs and live a full life outside of your role as an advisor, in return for advice that comes from a position of calm and contentment.

✓ **Choose your advice carefully.** Keep in mind that you are probably in a very different stage of life than the person you are talking to. Problems that you have mastered may not yet be on their radar. Put yourself in the other person's shoes by considering what crises you have gone through personally, but also in the context of your psychological development. What helped you get through them? Think of previous people you trusted and looked up to. Orient yourself to your idea of what made these people trusted persons and with what respect you were treated by them.

LATE ADULTHOOD: EGO INTEGRITY VS. DESPAIR

I generally refer to late adulthood as the last phase of life, which begins around retirement age and lasts until the end of life. In this phase, the self-image with which one approaches immediate crises and how one is able to react to feelings of helplessness is put to the test.

In late adulthood, one should be prepared to defend one's own dignity against all physical threats (e.g., physical weakness) and financial threats. The adult also now looks back on his or her life as a concatenation of multiple events and understands their interrelationships from a much deeper perspective, which is understood as the concept of ego integrity. The greatest challenge is to accept this for oneself, even in its shortcomings, and to settle feelings of remorse. With this realization comes an ultimate wisdom, which is defined by understanding one's own role in the world and the role of humanity as a whole. With the help of this wisdom, one is finally able to face death without fear and accept it as such.

The great weakness of humans at this point is being able to let things go - after all, we have learned so far that we always have the opportunity to revise our behavior and learn from our mistakes. However, we are often left with mistakes that we do not see from their ultimately helpful side, but deeply regret. For some, this mistake may be a disadvantageous professional decision, a persistent conflict with our children, or the loss of a loved one. In old age, however, it becomes virtually impossible to undo things. Those who nevertheless allow themselves to be overwhelmed by this desire run the risk of inwardly despairing of themselves. Self-esteem is undermined by this despair and, on the other hand, only increases an existing fear of death, since one sees it as the antagonist of one's unfulfilled desires and actively resists the actually desirable acceptance of one's own path in life. It is important to have a clear picture of oneself in order to counteract this fear and live a fulfilled life. Erikson's most memorable statement is that "He who learns as a child not to fear life will not fear death as an adult."

<u>Which is helpful at this stage:</u>

✓ **Accept the flaws in your life as a result of your actions.** Very few things on this planet are perfect. None of us is born an expert in life, but improvises where he knows no advice.

✓ You undoubtedly made decisions that in retrospect turned out to be good and right, but you couldn't have known that one hundred percent at the relevant moment. Reflect back on the factors that influenced your decision at the time. Understand your life as a long-term process and show forbearance for your younger self.

✓ **Make a list of the things you consider personal successes and personal failures.** It is well known that for every criticism we receive, we need at least five compliments to counteract the negative effect of insecurity. We feel the same way about the things we regret - we've developed tunnel vision and no longer see the successes that are actually worth celebrating. Keep in mind what you've accomplished in life so far and what it took to successfully overcome crises. By mentally reviewing the milestones of your life, perhaps some insights will emerge from a more confident perspective that will help you deal with the mistakes you have made. In fact, it is quite likely that you will begin to differentiate between unchangeable and changeable mistakes. Which these are, only you can judge - however, you always have the opportunity to call a certain person, live out a long-held passion, or take that trip you always shied away from in your younger years. Use your life experience to settle your past fears and have the courage to do something less than perfect, but take that step anyway.

What you can learn from inner conflicts throughout your life

Now you have gained a good overview of which inner conflicts dominate and influence our further development. Perhaps you recognize some crises you have already gone through and are just visualizing what kind of support you would have benefited most from at this point in your development. It would also be understandable if you felt a bit slain by the concept of "conflict" and now feel that life is one big battle to be fought with yourself. Erikson's model reads a bit like a bildungsroman in which the hero wages bitter battles and ponders philosophical questions until his head smokes.

Pause for a moment and recall the beginning of this guide, where it was explained that a clear delineation of developmental stages is more difficult than, say, studying trees or butterflies. Psychologists make do by observing people at certain ages and then identifying a central area of interest for a specific age. No doubt certain aspects of this theory will also be familiar to you through your own life experience, for example, that children develop particularly creative fears at a certain age, or that life upheavals also occur in adulthood, for example, through divorce, career changes, or the children moving out, which may require one to completely reorient and reinvent oneself. Perhaps your life so far has been a chain of very special and creative events, which do not correspond to a "classic" curriculum vitae. Perhaps you have never had to struggle with certain conflicts, but have struggled with other challenges that you felt you had been left alone with.

Think of the above guide much more as a fantastic journey. Sometimes you'll be accompanied by friends and confidants for years, but on some parts of the way it will seem as if you've been traveling alone for ages. Sometimes you'll meet interesting people who will challenge you and perhaps drive you up the wall. Most of the time you are on a wide, familiar path. At some points, however, a fork in the road arises, a winding, narrow path that you don't know and that may hold unknown dangers. You cannot know what awaits you at the other end of the path, and turning back later is bound to be a difficult undertaking. These two paths represent the eight conflicts that arise during your life, according to Erikson's model. The broad path symbolizes familiar situations and thought patterns. It is comfortable because it does not call for change, and it leads slowly downward because it can be an unexpected trap for you.

If you distrust people from the beginning, doubt your own abilities, actively isolate yourself and despair of your failures, you will eventually be alone. Your only option is to understand why the comfortable path is gradually becoming dangerous for you. As soon as a fork in the road opens up, consider stepping onto the unknown path. It takes some courage to show confidence when it has previously been disappointed elsewhere; to be proactive and take responsibility for your actions when you previously saw yourself as the play-thing of others; to say "no" and go your own way when you were previously seen as an always available support. Moreover, no one is asking you to change into a fundamentally optimistic and confident person when these character traits actually seem quite foreign to you. Finally, even Erikson acknowledges that our genetic makeup plays a role in our development, and a good portion of the population grows up as natural skeptics, which saves them from potential naiveté and exploitation.

You should not have to forget when other people have wronged you before - but if you put on an automatic protective armor, no one will get the chance to perhaps prove you exactly wrong. Erikson's distinction between two poles does not mean that a person should reach one of them perfectly. Rather, he understands each inner conflict in question as a scale like a personal test that you go through and at the end of which you get your result. Perhaps you trust in an average of 40% of all test situations and are therefore predominantly, but not fundamentally, distrustful. While this means that you can be open to other people, perhaps in return your attitude towards your own abilities may suffer because you distrust yourself.

In developmental psychology, there is the so-called self-assessment model of achievement motivation, in which a distinction is made between two types of people. One chooses realistically feasible tasks, attributes his success to his own performance and ability, and is generally satisfied with himself at the end of a task. Such people are called success-oriented people. The other, on the other hand, chooses either particularly easy or particularly difficult tasks in which the full capability potential is either barely exhausted or completely overloaded.

If the task was successfully accomplished, this person attributes his success to pure luck or chance; if the task was unsuccessful, the person shrugs and says, "I couldn't do it anyway." He is fundamentally dissatisfied with his own achievements, which is why such people are also called failure-oriented people. Why do failure-oriented people put themselves under such psychological pressure? They may never have learned to realistically assess their own abilities or have such a fear of failure that they would rather refuse a challenging situation than try and be less than perfect.

Such fears have something to do with a lack of trust in oneself. The point is: teaching people to trust themselves is much easier if you know how to trust other people. Most people who are hard on themselves on a regular basis would never talk that way to a friend who is in a similar situation. Slowly work your way up to projects and tasks you think you can conquer. Afterwards, be surprised by what you are capable of and take it a step further next time. You will be amazed at the personal peaks you can conquer if you have the courage to make the climb.

Remember that human development by no means ends when you enter adulthood. Every upheaval, every change in your life tests what you have learned so far and what support you receive in crisis situations. You remember well what you needed in your childhood and what you may never have gotten. Keep in mind the warning from the last phase of your life and don't regret missed opportunities that you can always make up for. Make sure that your personal environment gives back to you about as much as you give away on a daily basis. Good networks and long-lasting, intimate friendships are as important to your day-to-day psyche as seeking out new challenges, situations and people. Your brain still has a certain plasticity even at an advanced age and is accordingly quite receptive to new experiences. Seek stimulation outside your comfort zone and be aware that your self-esteem can endure failure and move past it with some maturity.

Take with you from Erikson's developmental model the insight that every challenge has at its core the opportunity for improvement. Some days you may be on the other end of a conflict that needs to be resolved, and you may be dealing with a young person who fundamentally rejects your beliefs and rules and absolutely refuses to listen to your persuasion. However, you know that your relationship is paramount in this. What matters is the extent to which you value and respect your counterpart as a human being, so that you are able to compromise or perhaps simply state your decision transparently and leave it at that. If your relationship has a strong foundation, it will survive any challenge and only become more unshakable through it.

Erikson took an optimistic view of life, repeatedly pointing out that no conflict is truly lost. Every conflict a child engages in is an opportunity to support that child with confidence and trust, and to witness their successes firsthand. By practicing leaving your adult perspective for a moment and taking a child's point of view, you will be much more likely to be able to help that child along in his or her insecurities and understand that he or she is not at all unfinished, but simply currently engaged in a different internal conflict than you are. Basically, you have this in common with every child.

Finally, remember Erikson's saying, with which he memorably summed up what is important in the upbringing of every human being: "Whoever learns as a child not to fear life, will not fear death as an adult." With this in mind, show your child that he or she can overcome his or her fears, and he or she will later be able to master them with confidence.